The Other Life

The Other Life

poems

Andrea Hollander

Story Line Press | *Pasadena, CA*

The Other Life
Copyright © 2000, 2021 by Andrea Hollander
All Rights Reserved

No part of this book may be used or reproduced in any manner whatsoever without the prior written permission of both the publisher and the copyright owner.

Grateful acknowledgement is made to the following magazines, which have published some of these poems: *Shiny*, *Texture*, *lower limit speech*, and *Exposures*.

ISBN 978-1-58654-117-0 (tradepaper)
978-1-58654-118-7 (casebound)

The National Endowment for the Arts, the Los Angeles County Arts Commission, the Ahmanson Foundation, the Dwight Stuart Youth Fund, the Max Factor Family Foundation, the Pasadena Tournament of Roses Foundation, the Pasadena Arts & Culture Commission and the City of Pasadena Cultural Affairs Division, the City of Los Angeles Department of Cultural Affairs, the Audrey & Sydney Irmas Charitable Foundation, the Kinder Morgan Foundation, the Meta & George Rosenberg Foundation, the Allergan Foundation, the Riordan Foundation, Amazon Literary Partnership, and the Mara W. Breech Foundation partially support Red Hen Press.

Second Edition
Published by Story Line Press
an imprint of Red Hen Press
www.redhen.org

Acknowledgments

Much appreciation to the editors of the following journals where some of these poems appeared, a few in different versions.

Atlanta Review: "Why I Married Him"
The Cortland Review: "What I Need It For," "What It Is"
Crab Orchard Review: "Happiness," "The Other Side of the Story," "Woman and Husband"
Crazyhorse: "My Father's Sweater"
DoubleTake: "The Hunters"
FIELD: "How It Is Done"
The Georgia Review: "An Explanation," "Burning the Letters," "Confessional Poet," "In Which Being Here Together Is Enough," "Love Song Ending with a Line by Horace"
The Hollins Critic: "Longing"
The Hudson Review: "Afterwards"
The Kenyon Review: "The Other Life," "Those Summer Sundays"
The Laurel Review: "Hunter, Gatherer"
The Midday Moon: "Pensioner, Leicester Square, London," "Poem Written at Home While You Fly over the Atlantic," "Spoken in a Voice that Could be His Own"
New England Review: "A Tree Like This One" (as "Gray")
Pendragon: "As If for No Other Reason," "What the Other Eye Sees"
Pivot: "Part of the Story"
Poet Lore: "What the Married Man Dreamed"
Poetry: "Goodness," "History," "Reading Aloud to My Mother"
Rhino: "In This Poem You Refuse To Speak"
Shenandoah: "A Way of Speaking," "On the Other Side of the World," "Storms"
Solo: "Gray"
The Southern California Anthology: "How He Warmed Himself"
Tar River Poetry: "May 29" (as "Trying Not To Listen")

"What the Other Eye Sees," "As If for No Other Reason," and "A Way of Speaking" appeared in *What the Other Eye Sees* (Wayland Press, 1991) and "In This Poem You Refuse to Speak" in Living on the Cusp (Moonsquilt Press, 1981), limited edition chapbooks. "How He Warmed Himself" was awarded 3rd prize in the Ann Stanford Poetry Prize competition. "The Hunters" is anthologized in *And What Rough Beast: Poems at the End of the Century* (Ashland Poetry Press, 1999) and "Storms" in *Buck and Wing: Southern Poetry at the Millennium* (Washington and Lee University Press, 2000).

I am grateful to the National Endowment for the Arts and the Arkansas Arts Council for generous fellowships, and to Lyon College for the time to write and the opportunity to teach what I love. Gratitude to Martha Collins, Stephen Corey, Deborah Cummins,

Kathleen Lynch, Fred Marchant, Virginia Wray, and especially to David Jauss for valuable insights. Thanks, too, to Rockshop and Buzz members. A writer could not have better intellectual and emotional support than I've received from my husband, Todd, and my son, Brooke, my first readers, who provided excellent and sensitive feedback on poems in progress.

Stanley W. Lindberg (1939 – 2000) of *The Georgia Review* was my first editor. Each of these poems is testament to the enormous power of his encouragement in those early years. He is very much missed.

For Todd and Brooke, always—

And for

Milton and Evelyn Hollander
Don and Isabelle Budy

Contents

What the Other Eye Sees   13

❦

Those Summer Sundays   17
Goodness   18
In Which Being Here Together Is Enough   19
Love Song Ending with a Line by Horace   21
Why I Married Him   23
Poem Written at Home
    While You Fly over the Atlantic   24
The Hunters   26
Wound   27
Reading Aloud to My Mother   28
A Tree Like This One   29
History   30
Pensioner, Leicester Square, London   31
How He Warmed Himself   32
My Father's Sweater   34
What It Is   36
The Other Life   38
Longing   40
Afterwards   42
The Other Side of the Story   43
What the Married Man Dreamed   44
Part of the Story   45
Happiness   46
Delta Flight 1152   48

On the Other Side of the World	50
Hunter, Gatherer	51
An Explanation	52
Burning the Letters	54
Woman and Husband	56
May 29	57
What I Need It For	58
As If for No Other Reason	59
Storms	60
Gray	62
Spoken in a Voice That Could Be His Own	63
In This Poem You Refuse to Speak	64
A Way of Speaking	65
Writing This Poem	67
Confessional Poet	69
How It Is Done	72
Notes	73

One's real life is so often the life that one does not lead.
—Oscar Wilde

One less hope becomes
One more song.
—Anna Akhmatova

What the Other Eye Sees

And I lie sleeping with one eye open,
Hoping
That nothing, nothing will happen.
—Mark Strand

It sees half a woman,
the muse of the storm
still searching its center,
that room that does not move,
around which the house collapses.

It sees half a moon,
the shadow's steep staircase,
the half where the deep sea
pitches the body afterwards
and the broken shells of dreams.

It sees half a life,
the half you write about,
the half you have not yet lived
but calculate its measurements:
its snake-like length, its ribbon

of deaths, its long unfurling
possibilities.

The Other Life

Those Summer Sundays

Sundays my father would join us
at the club pool, his skin
white and delicate as cigarette paper

on the one day he took
from the women who lined
his waiting room

month after month.
I waited at the shallow end.
He rose from the board

and dropped
straight as a table knife
without a splash. Always

the women stared, women
from whose bodies he had pulled
daughters, released sons.

And never
would he surface
until he had maneuvered through the depths

to the place where I stood. Giddy, I would close
my eyes as he hoisted me
from the flawless water

on his shoulders, the two of us
one thing, perfect and tall.
I did not know then

of the sometimes dangerous
entrances of men, how some will lift
what others slowly drown.

Goodness

As my husband set the table for breakfast,
I stood at the kitchen counter in my pink chenille bathrobe,
its pockets worn through, waiting for the toast to rise,

and realized that this, too, I would lose—
this moment so routine
it would soon disappear into the daily machine of our lives

like the beautiful pebble I dropped on the beach
and moments later couldn't find.
As good as it was to be home in this good house

with my husband humming something familiar,
the tea already steeping, the juice poured, even the butter
waiting in its porcelain plate on the table,

there was nothing I would remember it by, and I knew it.
If the phone had rung with bad news about my father
even the way the sun angled onto the rug would have brought

the bad news back again each time,
and I could never have worn the bathrobe again.
Is this why Anne Frank's diary matters?

At another place, another time,
the life of a thirteen-year-old girl would have disappeared
into a box in the upstairs closet,

a few pages of it read, perhaps, by her grown-up son, and then
because he had to drive his daughter to school
and pick up the paper on the way, he would have closed it,

promising himself to someday read the rest, then whistled
down the stairs in his herringbone vest and jacket
to where his daughter waited in the sunlit hall.

In Which Being Here Together Is Enough

Candlelight flickered
all night

while a ceaseless moth
outside the cabin

pressed against the cold
window, its wings

outstretched,
beating.

Only after we finished
and drifted

on our rumpled bed
and the waxy heat

of the candle sank
into itself,

nearly quenched,
no longer a flame

but a waning filament,
did the moth,

exhausted but persistent,
find its way in

and with its wings
extinguish

the diminished light
and become itself

extinguished. Our separate
breaths grew even,

singular,
the night air thinned,

and later
daylight entered

lightly as a moth
and at a cost

to no one.

Love Song Ending with a Line by Horace

What the eye sees
with its magic attachments
when you look at him
and he looks back

What the ear hears
when its words are not words at all
but the wild birds
of another's heart

What the mouth knows
but cannot speak

What the cheek feels
when the lashes of his eyes
play upon it
a secret music

When the limbs sigh
as the body lies
anticipating

And the mouth knows
but cannot speak

And the hands—
the hands that want
everything
for themselves
and won't be spared
and won't be told
to stop

And the mouth knows
but will not speak

What the heart has had
no fingers of any hand
will hold

Why I Married Him

In front of the whole class
when I stopped mid-sentence, lost
for a single word, silence
pushing its way in, unstoppable
as a wave, my mind like a sunbather
weary from the heat of the beach, asleep
in the constant glare, the sea's drone
masking the sea's approach,
waves moving imperceptibly closer,
about to take over,

he found it, the lifeguard who had sat quietly
all summer long, more looked at
than looking, found and shoved
the right word into the right place
like a wall built to keep the sea out,
and saved me.

And I knew that with him life would be
like that. Even on the calmest days
he'd stay up on his ten-foot chair
watching, ready to hold
even the ocean back.

Poem Written at Home
While You Fly over the Atlantic

When you were small I'd try
to wake you without being heard—a breeze
barely disturbing your hair, a bit of sunlight

on your shoulder. I wanted you to assume
you had stirred on your own,
that I had appeared

by a kind of ordinary magic. Or
sung you to sleep
and stayed.

Today I look out at these trees
and imagine the sky
looks down upon them

as a mother would
with their seasonal changes
it anticipates and prepares for.

It is merely backdrop, after all,
even with its two bodies
that illuminate everything.

From the airplane window
you look out now at the blackness
you can't touch, yet which holds you

in its perfect, invisible arms
and will deliver you
onto this earth (I must believe)

as I once did, watching you emerge
out of my singular body
whole and alive and on your way

for the first time
someplace important
without me.

The Hunters

Dressed in their green spotted drabs to blend in
with trees, my brother and his new friends, then
nineteen, erected their dark tents and dug
a latrine, then gathered twigs from the edge

of their camp and the driest leaves, and at
twilight all of them assembled, then bent
their heads for a moment over their Tang
or their coffee or tea, and one boy sang

a little prayer in the unarmed quiet
(at night sometimes my brother still sings it),
and even the air began to settle
except for the occasional rattle

of insects and in the nearby distance
mortar fire from Da Nang, insistent.

Wound

When you asked if I wanted to see
and I said yes, you opened your robe,
lifted off the gauze, and exposed
a barbed wire fence cut
through a field of snow.
The snow wasn't white exactly
but used or forgotten, the air
hardened by winter so that
to breathe was to choke.
And along its black length
that separated into two
your past and your future,
that fence was streaked
with indecipherable detritus
as though some small animal
had been dragged from its life into it
and died there, its clots of fur
still frozen in the barb.
This is your chest, I told myself,
not some deserted pasture
flattened by winter over
what is lost or missing.
I should have closed my eyes
or pictured the ocean instead.
Twenty-seven years after your death
I still can't turn away. I shut my eyes
and see your chest stitched closed.
If only poems were the only places
to know such cold.

Reading Aloud to My Mother

After dinner on those last days
we hoped would linger

until the thinning moon rose
into the numb sky,

I sat beside her bed
and read from the novel she'd begun

months before on her own.
At first the words wouldn't leave

the page. Then, like crows
nibbling invisible debris

on the uneven horizon long enough
to grow invisible themselves,

they unpredictably
lifted all at once above it

and pushed across the darkening sky,
a tribe of inky letters

on a page that itself was slowly growing black
until the words, there or not, were mute

as the new moon that in a few days
would rise and fall again in the black sky

and I would be there and watching
and would not see it.

A Tree Like This One

Once, when my mother was alive
and the Russian olive tree in the backyard not yet
blown over by the storm, and we lay awhile

under it on a blanket, feeling lazy, looking
up into the gray of its leaves,
teasing one another

not at all like mother and daughter
but two friends who had poked
pins into their index fingers and had sworn

by the blood, we decided to pretend
that, like her grandparents, we had walked
all night through a forest to get there

and taken everything important
with us, everything
we could carry, that is,

having buried the copper pots
and taken the Seder dish,
but thinking, too,

that her grandparents would have walked
out under a tree just like this one, pretending
they had already arrived

in the New World, that this
was only a picnic, after all,
here on the uneven grass

that a little way off they could hear
my mother and me
already alive and giggling.

History

What if there hadn't been that one
moment when a man came home
and said to his wife, "No,
we will not leave that way, made to go
off someplace to work. I heard some talk. I know."

And what if there hadn't been that one
word, *know*, that his wife knew
to be the truth, the way the heart knows when blue
is really black disguised as blue, a bruise
cruelly thicker than it seems, news
that the dead were her own blood, and she knew
when they said they'd be safe that something truly
dark was speeding through.

And what if there hadn't been that one
night when even making love wasn't
safe enough, when, though the depot was crowded with cousins
and friends, the man and woman lied, said "visitors," said "Russian"
to the right smileless face, walked instead of running
to the other waiting train, watched as the landscape ran out, then
the sea, then all that was ahead of them, nearly crushing
each other with love, but never speaking it.

Thank God, thank love, thank even terror—that one
seed already in place, my mother.

Pensioner, Leicester Square, London

My heart tightened when I saw him
shivering alone on a stoop

but I did not stop. I walked by nodding, smiling,
hoping he'd take what I'd given,

hoping that when I returned
he'd be gone.

Later I thought
the heart is born to singing, even alone.

Even in its tiny despair
it earns its place

high in its own steeple.
For isn't despair a song,

rich and singular as prayer?
And don't the gods, too, have hearts?

Or do they smile
only on the one who stops, who hears

the thin tune, dull and off key,
who enters

the locked church of another,
who kneels and sings along.

How He Warmed Himself

All night the wind railed in the trees.
Their father closed the windows tightly as he could
against the noise, and, assured they were asleep, crunched out,

quietly as possible, into the snow-packed world,
too soon for shoveling, too late
for anything else.

He must have thought himself invisible
in that white world
or small and doomed

beneath his own canopy of breath
that must have somehow seemed
a separate thing.

As he lifted the garage door and clunked it down again
against the muffled light, and slipped
the key into the ignition, and turned it,

he must have thought past them,
past the photographs arranged chronologically on the hallway wall
and all their pastels on the refrigerator,

past the summer days that grew lazily green on the other side
of the world he could not reach, or wait for.
He must have settled in and warmed himself

against the winter storm stacking its white cache against one side
of the house, his own chronic storm
waning inside him,

against the furniture they still owed money on
and the car itself, against his unheld rage
that rested now like a shriveled thread on the dashboard.

He must have warmed himself
against the lingering bit of restlessness or second thoughts,
and the blackness they knew nothing of

that crowded in, against even
these words he couldn't guess he'd cause,
and all the other wordless deeds

the dead give birth to.

My Father's Sweater

It was snug on him anyway, she said,
his wife, my stepmother, when she offered it
like a monthly magazine already read,

nothing she would miss if I took it,
something to keep me
warm in the bitter afternoon of late

March, to turn my thoughts from the empty bed
where she said he had lain for a week.
She hadn't phoned. She kept

believing he'd recover, that he'd guide her
down the hospital corridor
to their car as he'd done before,

my sleek father who'd kept slipping
into childhood, my brilliant daddy with only
saliva on his tongue.

How the worn wool glowed, how its burgundy twill
warmed me as if it were the wine
of the same name and I had had my fill.

I folded the sleeves at the wrists, pushed them up like
small accordions.
All the way home on the plane, I lay back

in my window seat surrounded
by the sad comfort of his familiar redolence.
Ten years later I'm astounded

I never wore it again. Not once have I lifted it
from the closet shelf where it lies
in the pungence of cedar, out of sight

like the soldier my father had been
in the forests of Germany, the charred
chateaux of France, where he had hidden

his fear like a stolen radio, its voices foreign
but alive, indecipherable and distant
as now his own voice has grown,

inscrutable as faith,
insistent
as the long absence of his breath.

What It Is

It is
whatever it is
that stirs the house

of your heart,
that shares
your hunger,

your thirst,
your urge all day
to hear more

than your own voice
voicing its foolishness.

It is
whatever it is
in your hands

that slithers away,
whatever can only be
glimpsed, sudden

or sharp, but tuneless,
bass notes, not
melody.

You were born
knowing

you'd have to learn
whatever it would take
and even to learn

what to make of it.
It is not
the words

in your throat
not even
your honest intention.

When you open
your mouth

it is
whatever it is
that no longer speaks

that longs to speak,
whatever it is
that trembles.

The Other Life

The life you wish you had lived
inhabits the lavender scarf
you lift now and then

from the dresser drawer.
Like perfume, it invades
every room in your house

with possibilities
until your body is filled—
that body

anyone can touch.
It holds on tight
the way on an autumn afternoon

the fig tree loses
only its leaves and not
the fruits that have turned

in on themselves
like tiny fists.
Must you give up

this life, whose doors
you have dreamed open?
Though you have parted

its curtains, worn
its moonlit glow?
Haven't you earned

this grief that makes you
unable to breathe
anything else?

These are the days you linger
at the dinner table eating
nothing, the other life

wanting you only
to want it,
to keep it known,

an initialed handkerchief
without an owner.
It is palpable

as that tiny mahogany chest
made to hold letters
you wish you'd received,

or that diary whose empty pages
have already yellowed.
Or your heart, which beats

only in the other life, the life
you covet and protect,
the one you invent and invent

because it invents you back.

Longing

Every word I write is made of it.
A small boat of popsicle sticks saved all summer

and glued together by a child
is stuck in the rushes.

There are woods in which I have never walked
and perfume in those woods.

Even if I could go there
I wouldn't be able to find its source.

I say this: if words could be laid down,
if they could be held,

my longing would end.
But words are not what they say.

They echo only the sound
of a voice, a remnant, itself

an echo. They sting
and disappear like the beautiful

hornet whose nest is nearby—
that quick, that painful.

Some words undo me—your name,
for example, or the words you write. You

who are both lifeboat and line,
if you were here now

I would touch
and touch you and never have enough.

If the rushes let go, that boat will break up
and travel unrecognizable

stick by stick in the tide.

Afterwards

Shy, she leans away from him and sighs, thinks
the way the neon sign blinks off and on
through the curtains—gold and blue, gold and blue—
is a sign of something larger than themselves.

He fiddles with her hair, gets up the nerve
to hum a tune he knows she likes, endures
her unresponsive back, observes
the curtains changing colors with the lights.

Talking in bed ought to be easiest—
but silence, that untameable weed, thick
and uncrushable as passion, flourishes between
them now, numb at the mattress's separate edges,

her prom dress upright and stiff in the corner
standing on its layers of crinolines
as though she ordered it there, as though
the girl who had danced in it hours before had not yet left,

as though his tux folded on the chair and the pair
of cufflinks side by side on the table meant business,
as though, after all, it wasn't their bodies that mattered
nor the months the two of them had planned this hour.

What words could she use to erase all this and return
to the night before when she modeled for her father
showing him where her corsage would go and where
tomorrow she would pin the boutonnière?

The Other Side of the Story

*When you reach my age, you begin to remember
the truth of things.*
—Esther Hollander, age 91

Ever since I could tell it, I've told this side
even to myself, the one that could have been

photographed, frame by frame. In which he carried me
through the doorway and onto the bed, in which

though the fire blazed, the heat in the room was something
the two of us created, never mind it was November,

the shutters on the windows frozen shut, never mind
we were practically children, both nineteen.

I've told the story so many times I thought I'd forget
the other side, blurred for years in my private mirror,

though now the glass has cleared, and I see precisely
how cold it was that first time in the cabin on the lake,

and how long he took to build the fire.
That it went out quickly, that he tried a few more times,

then let it die. I saw that he was clumsy.
Without his shirt his chest was pale, his arms thin.

How much it hurt when he entered. And after he'd fallen asleep,
how I stared at my skirt and blouse

folded over the back of the chair, and the logs
barely charred in the open fireplace. I see that room

so clearly now, how small and barren it was
and how insignificant.

What the Married Man Dreamed

Though he sensed he was only dreaming,
he lay back on the bed, watched her unpack,

watched as she turned and grappled
with the fact of his being there. Whether or not

she knew she was someone he'd only invented
for the night, someone he needed finally in a room

like this, motel or not, she moved toward him,
lay down beside his body, touched his face.

That was all there was, all there had to be.
Dream or not, it was something to keep,

the way her electricity spread
through him, under them the bed

fully made, all their clothes on, her skirt
not even lifted, and, except his heart,

nothing in his life disturbed.

Part of the Story

> *Just leaning toward someone is part of the story.*
> —William Stafford

Though she may not even remember
the way his arm felt pressed against hers,

he remembers. In bed with his wife sometimes
he imagines her body instead. He says her name

only to point out how plain she is, how bored
she'd make the unlucky man who had to

endure her. Weekdays he drives the routine
streets to work. He brushes by her desk, borrows

a paper clip, a stack of envelopes. He thinks
how safe this is. Leaning toward someone

is only part of the story, the way his arm felt
pressed against hers, the center.

Happiness

It's a kind of fairy tale
my friend, the writer, tells me—
a beautiful castle

but impossible to live in.
And yet I recognize
how happiness invents

a life. Like those flitters
of dust in a sunlight beam,
it enters a man's house

late in the afternoon,
surveys his room, refuses
to settle.

Once upon a time a beautiful woman
stared at the paintings
that line his walls,

acknowledged his back
as he sat at his desk
for hours, creating her.

He wrote and rewrote his careful lines,
insisted she have a single birthmark,
an unexplained scar.

He fed her
an orange, peeled away
the loops of skin, removed the sections,

each one a separate
universe of sweetness,
and watched as she let her tongue

learn the shape of everything
he gave her. She filled
his pages.

Happiness is to enter this room
and recognize the odor
of orange and woman mixed,

to fall in love with the way
remembrance and invention
trick the heart

and the way, even on paper,
a woman's presence
can enter a room

and create a kind of bliss,
her scent entering his
phrases, then his sentences,

her blouse on the floor beside his shoes,
her brassiere undone,
and everything in the real world safe,

his wife aloof, or at least upstairs,
the sunlight growing bright and on the move,
then fading.

Delta Flight 1152

After the first drink, you can be
what you're not. It's so easy, all you must do

is answer this man's questions with truths
you've just invented—*on my way to the annual meeting*

of master magicians, or to a conference of physicists
or international bankers—and your life is enviable,

new. Tell him you're sad because you're on your way
to your sister's wedding and you're in love

with her fiancé. Wipe your eyes,
sigh, mention almost under your breath the baby

you had to give up, the job. You're the one
who introduced them, you couldn't stop yourself, he would come

to your desk at the office. How lonely he was,
how young. But if you reveal the afternoon

of lunch on the rooftop, how for you
it wasn't enough, there's certain danger

this man, his drink finished, ice diluted
in the bottom of his plastic cup, will lean too far

into your invented life. He'll offer his handkerchief.
You'll finger his embroidered initials. He'll touch your arm,

hand you his card. His voice unsteady,
he'll tell you to call him at home—you,

an only child on her way
to see the ocean for the first time. You, who have managed

to live a moral life, whose troubled heart has never
surrendered, now with your wild and dangerous

lies, you could turn toward this stranger
and open.

On the Other Side of the World

He was dancing again
with the other man's wife, while her husband dozed

in the boozy room. The music moaned from its little box
in the corner. The dancers swayed a little closer.

We were all tipsy. In the kitchen women giggled.
The odor of coffee rose.

I sat on the couch tired of trying to chat
in a language I didn't own,

making over and over
the same mistakes. The music faded, his hand

now on the small of her back, hers
on the back of his neck, their feet

barely moving, the weight of what would come next
shifting right, then left.

And where were you, my love? I stood at the window
on the other side of the world

and observed the predictable
moon, that ravaged, over-used philanderer's tool.

Like me, it kept its place, barely visible
in the otherwise unmarked heavens.

Hunter, Gatherer

When he speaks to a woman, he soothes her
stockings down. Not with his hands. His fingers
stay in plain view on a table, say, or

stroke his own face, having both less and more
to do in this distraction he creates
while his resourceful baritone (that hates

the very clothes he loves) convinces her
to undress herself, undo her bra, lower
her panties. His voice is the actual

desired object. Subtle, sexual
(he's practiced this), he stops speaking, let's some
silence linger between them. She wants him

then, wants his sound in her, to be bitten
by it. She opens her mouth, breathes him in.

An Explanation

> *Frank was missing something, and women would do anything
> to find out what it was.*
> —James Salter

It's nothing, really, just a kind of trick I use
to keep them. I look up from their bodies

with a tenderness I've maintained after we've made love
wishing to extend even further

that welcome moment of grace that settles in
just after the inevitable diminishment

over which neither of us has any control.
I look up from their bodies and glance

toward a window, if there is a window,
or a closet door or a calendar on the wall, perhaps

a candle on the bedside table with its rarefied flame.
If there's a painting above the bed, I make sure it's safe

before we even begin to undress or lie down
to undress one another. Once

it was one of those portraits of Jesus
naked and bleeding, which ruined everything.

I'm all there when I'm there. Yet sometimes, I've learned,
it's better to lift them out of themselves by giving

a little bit less. I don't mean to be cruel,
cutting them off from my pure attention. I only want

the deepest they'll give me, the thing you can't ask for—
they don't know where it is themselves. I think

of Valentino who was forced to use only his eyes to speak
and his body, the sound of his voice kept irretrievably

from us, that incomplete circle that wanted finishing,
and we, of course, supplied the best.

That's it, really. Leaving something necessary
out that they'll fill in. Something small, of course,

but important, something at first you don't withhold
so they'll notice right away when you do.

Remember the page in the children's magazine
that displayed a kitchen or a yard and asked you to find

the ten things wrong? An upside-down
clock, say, or a dog in a tree?

It's taken me years to learn this, and it works.
A woman will nest herself for as long as I want her.

She gives me more and more of everything, tries
to fill my gaps, plug holes in my conversation.

When she finally tires of her own failures, and leaves,
it never hurts. I always have at least her sympathies

and her longing. There are so many beautiful women
lighting this world. It's the only way I've found

to possess them.

Burning the Letters

This was before they were married,
before she understood what he had done
to her heart, before she understood
that she had let him. His words meant something

before she understood what he had done.
He stood beside her at the stainless steel sink.
She let his words mean something—
their thick current, the blame she'd accepted.

He stood beside her at the sink
and lit the first page, turned it to flame.
Its thick current, the bruise she'd expected,
passed through her. The words she'd written

lit the first page and turned it to flame.
The stack was nine inches thick, copies
of the words she'd written
for other men—words to herself, really.

The stack was thick with copious
marks on paper her heart had made
for other men, words from her, real
words he wanted to end.

The marks her heart had made
he wanted turned to ash, page by page.
He wanted them to end like this:
black on white, blue light, orange flame,

page after violent page turned to ash
until there was nothing at all, not one page,
black or white. Blue flame, orange light—
what had defined her no longer saved.

Then there was nothing at all, not even rage.
Her heart stood vacant before him—
it neither defined nor saved her.
This was before they were married.

Woman and Husband

The fray between us over, spilled and mopped,
this bed a shoreline finally reached, he stops
explaining, stops my mouth as well, and with
his chest against my back, his breath
familiar in my hair, insists
on silence. The clock is all we hear: it ticks,
we breathe. The hickory near our window
vibrates gold, our door is closed,
the sun ignites the clock. Is it enough
to turn and kiss his mouth?
Or will I feed on air that someone else
has breathed? Or taste what she spit out? Enough.
I remember when I first conceived him in my life.
I craved the softness of his voice, his eyes
that penetrated mine. Disease
is made of less.
How soon the sun will leave the clock, the trees
brush grayish tremblings on the chest of drawers.
His breath is heavy at the hollow of my neck.
What mercifulness this is. A gift—
a broken gift
I'm finally willing to give back.

May 29

After the divorce papers are signed
and she has looked one more time
at him, the way, when she was five,

she was forced to look at Grandma
and say goodbye, his body strange
in the herringbone suit she knows

he must have borrowed
like the look he wore all day
sitting gravely with his lawyer

as if that too were something
worn on such occasions then
returned or given away.

And after she has stayed
in the ladies' room long enough for him
to shake the hands of other men

and slip through the revolving doors
and down the steps, whole
into the open day

where, for him, the world was made
the way the world was made
when she was ten

and sat on her father's shoulders and only
the clowns on stilts were taller,
then she, too, exits

from the gray, unremarkable building, out
into the rest of her life, its new
cotton flowered dress, its new shoes.

What I Need It For

I meant it for my desk, to hold my pencils and pens,
but I need flowers instead, yellow-centered
summer daisies to bluster into my poems.

Each morning when I trudge into my study,
rain or shine, rain or (mostly) more rain,
one look at these white pinwheels

each with its own little sun, and I can begin
to believe my own weather is different.
But what if you stepped into that room

just now, awkward as our first day, hesitant
and wordless? The flowers could have been
roses, of course. Better they aren't. Better

they are common flowers, the kind
you plant only once,
and year after year they return.

As If for No Other Reason

The moon is up
to throw its light on the line

where a woman has forgotten
to take down her wash.

The light on her porch
has been broken for weeks.

She's cursed the kids who did it
and that no-good man who left

a stone in her belly.
Her hair's still in curlers.

Her rocking chair creaks.
The moon sends her pictures

of sheets and underwear.
She'd like to throw stones

at the next man who speaks
or at the moon

or the old dog across the street
who used to chase cars,

who barks in his sleep
and pees on everything

or at me
for keeping my own light on.

Storms

*Think of the storm roaming the sky uneasily
like a dog looking for a place to sleep in,
listen to it growling.*
   —Elizabeth Bishop

After her tired dogs
retreat, the mangrove keys

settle back to sleep. Though thunder
shakes the palms,

it's from a distance so harmless
a bird looks up

only occasionally, his feet stuck
in the lazy water.

My storms are
wild cats screaming from the trees,

the winds
silent at first, then stiff, vicious,

taking the roofs with them.
My trees won't calm themselves

nor birds betray
their hidden places. Here, rain is never

truly welcome. Even when weeds
grow dry as chalk and the dog

won't leave the air-conditioned room,
I'd rather have the dust.

Think of me sleeping some night
in a tent along the river, lulled at first

by those early drops.
When all at once the ground

becomes a river, too, think of me
lucky to get out. This time

think of me lucky.

Gray
for Andrew Engborg

When it looks as though the day will finally be
sunny, I mourn a little for the clouds
that didn't come, or the squall,

and when the daffodils rise
open-faced one morning in March
in an orderly row,

some small stone sinks in the pool of me
and the ripples along the surface signal
a letting go I didn't want.

Though I moved on purpose to this place
where summer lingers by inching
like a stain into autumn and spring, where winter

rattles only briefly in white-face,
some human truth
streaking through the grease paint,

these days it's only haze I love,
unnameable weather,
an uneventful sky that resembles despair but isn't,

its grayness insisting gray is all there is,
a smudged newsprint that erases the news,
a calming absence which removes for awhile

the absence of you, child, and the accident that left
just your mother alive. She strapped you snug in your car seat
and kissed your head, and then the sun grew brilliant

and wild on the highway's edge.

Spoken in a Voice That Could Be His Own

In the living room I sit, touch
the piano keys, polish
each one smooth, follow the slow scales

that climb, that calm me. I want the rails
of the banister to lead me
up to the third floor where I'll be

that boy who suffered fright
when his father's uniform fit,
but felt his warmth, his soft

yes, his permanence. I ought
to know this room—peach walls, white trim,
mahogany piano, slim

man in the antique mirror there.
He should be me. He's not. A car
stops in the drive. Is the woman

walking through the door my wife? Can
I forget her face? My mother
swore we live a single life. Her

own was brief. I know I know my
hands. The clock has hands. I tie my
tie to memorize the steps. She

kisses me. I love her eyes, keys
I cannot lose, truths I believe in.
Somewhere in rapture grief begins.

In This Poem You Refuse to Speak

Instead a river rushes by, snaps
your losses. The words you might have used
tumble in the froth, a few
surfacing now and then,
snagged at the bank for at least
one season: clumps of leaves
caught on rock.

Bend down. There is no mirror here.
And not quite music
or silence, though silence might be this:
the gurgling monotony of river frogs,
of voiceless boats moored to the distance.
Or simply the water itself
disclaiming your life.

Why stop here? What's to learn?
And why put your faith in one river
so far south it never freezes, so wide
you're not all that's swiftly lost?
If you did speak you'd lie.
Even before you take off your clothes
you disappear inside.

A Way of Speaking

of saying hello
to everything that deserves
notice, even while it

hides: ice patterns
scarcely seen behind
the shower curtain

on the inside
of the bathroom window,
or wild

grass pushed up
along that unseeable line it finds
between the parking lot

and Sears, the way
the mouth stays open
while the sleeper sleeps, and moves

sometimes and makes
undecipherable sounds,
the way hands

close tight around
a blanket fold,
steering you

through the world you're
in now, the one where
you speak

invisibly, as a poem
tries to do, travelling
to a lost place,

and everyone who hears it
finally home.

Writing This Poem

This is a poem
in my own voice with its odd
pitch and ordinary vocabulary.

It is a poem
in the language I speak, the one
with too many questions

and apologies for its narrow
sidewalks, its one open
sky which is never

the blue I describe yet always
enormous with its singular
moon and the moon's

sad take on everything human.
When it sees my face closing in,
this poem sometimes

backs away
the way a man once did,
a man I thought I loved

and did love,
or the way that same man one day
finally kissed me

on my cheek—which means
exactly what you think it means.
When I sleep, I dream

the poem's dream. When I wake
I try to walk through the world
as only a person would,

no longer haunted.
Hunted, the poem leads me
to the last row

where no one else sits, where it hums
a different tune in my ear,
softly at first, with hesitation,

and finally distracts me
into its particular melody,
tempting me toward the perpetual

pen in my purse,
the voracious white spaces
in the playbill's margins,

that world where I live that only
writing this poem
makes real.

Confessional Poet

Sometimes when I read my poems
I think only about the dinner to come,

about the Chardonnay and the gaze
of my host, the way he will study me

across the table's white ironed cloth
and tapered candle, and the way

I'll consider his mouth, his lips. So,
I apologize. I confess. As you listen,

I may be someplace else, though my voice
does the work you expect, my mouth

rounded over the words they express,
my lips poised at the edge

of my muted consonants, my suitable vowels.
And though we are together

in this small auditorium or lecture hall or
classroom or café, already I have betrayed you

as easily as I used to betray
the congregation at church. At sixteen

I would open my mouth to sing
all those solemn hymns to Jesus

as I clocked in at the job
of making my face do one thing,

my mind another. I portrayed
one of the earnest,

my pure face invoking the presumption
of sinlessness, the countenance

of belief. But while I sang
I conjured the minister

without his robes,
sidling up behind me, pressing

his nonsectarian body against mine.
Oh, I was a sinner,

at least in thought—the same thing
according to my Catholic friends.

Now I stand at a lectern and confess
everything—the lies I have lived or invented,

the truths I have hidden in them.
I describe in detail the delicate

fruits of the forbidden and all the ways
I have enjoyed them—

the fruits themselves and the telling,
that other way to taste them again.

Fellow sinners, as I mouth these words
I want you to believe,

I am imagining another place
I've never been, another lover

I will bring to life, another journey
on which I could take you, another trip

on which I will never otherwise go.

How It Is Done

You go inside, take off your shoes,
enter the room everyone else believes is too dark,
open the small drawer of the ebony desk
your father brought back from his year in Japan
with its carved heads and torsos of dragons and serpents—
so many your mother sent it to the cellar.
You take out the pen and the bottle
of India ink, black as the dragons' ebony eyes,
then from the back the sheaf of paper, so white
it is new snow against the window the day
the power lines were downed by the storm.
For a long time you look through that window,
and finally make your way out of that room,
that house. You walk without considering the hidden
existence of sidewalks or the carless streets. You are careless.
You tunnel through drifts or climb them,
and you keep on like this until it snows enough
to hide your way back, as you are doing now,
one word at a time.

Notes

"Those Summer Sundays" is in response to Robert Hayden's "Those Winter Sundays."

Line 9 of "Afterwards" is from Philip Larkin's "Talking in Bed."

"An Explanation" is in response to Stephen Dunn's "Missing."

The first line of "What I Need It For" is a variation on one from Stephen Sandy's "A Bamboo Brushpot."

"Woman and Husband" is in the voice of the woman of Robert Lowell's "Man and Wife."

Biographical Note

Andrea Hollander is the author of five full-length poetry collections and the recipient of numerous honors and awards, including two Pushcart Prizes (poetry and literary nonfiction) and two fellowships from the National Endowment for the Arts. In 2011, after more than three decades living in the Arkansas Ozark Mountains, where she ran a bed and breakfast for fifteen years and served as the Writer-in-Residence at Lyon College for twenty-two, she moved to Portland, Oregon, where she founded the Ambassador Writing Seminars. Her website is www.andreahollander.net.